Introduction:

- Presentation of Sardinia as an island with a rich winemaking tradition and unique identity.
- Historical context of wine production in Italy and Sardinia's place in this scenario.
- Geographic and climatic characteristics of the island: influence of the Mediterranean, winds, soils.
- Production overview: cultivated grapes, diversity of wines, challenges and potential.

History of Viticulture in Sardinia:

- Origins of viticulture on the island: influence of the Phoenicians, Romans and other peoples.
- Traditions and customs related to wine in Sardinian culture.
- Evolution of production over the centuries: challenges and achievements.
- Influence of different cultures and dominations on Sardinian winemaking.
- Wine production in modern Sardinia: tradition and innovation.

Terroir Sardo:

- Influence of the Mediterranean climate: sun, wind, temperature variations.
- Diversity of soils and microclimates on the island.
- Sardinia wine regions and their characteristics.
- Importance of terroir in defining the typicality of wines.

Sardinian Grapes:

- Indigenous varieties:
  - Tintas: Cannonau, Carignano, Monica, Bovale Sardo, Girò.
  - Brancas: Vermentino, Nuragus, Vernaccia di Oristano.
- Characteristics and potential of each variety.
- Importance of preserving native grapes.
- Other varieties grown on the island.

Wine Production:

- Vineyard management: adaptation to climatic conditions and soil types.
- Winemaking techniques: traditional and modern methods.
- Elaboration of different styles of wine: reds, whites, rosés, sparkling wines, fortified wines.
- The search for identity and typicality in Sardinian wines.
- The role of the winemaker in expressing terroir.

Appellations of Origin:

- Italian wine classification system: DOCG, DOC, IGT.
- Main designations of origin in Sardinia: Vermentino di Gallura DOCG, Cannonau di Sardegna DOC, etc.
- Regulations and specificities of each denomination.
- Table wines and production "outside" appellations.

Sardinian Wines:

- Sensory profiles of wines: aromas, flavors, structure, body.
- Detailed descriptions of the island's wines, highlighting their characteristics.
- Pairing with Sardinian cuisine.

- Tips for tasting and appreciation.
- Important labels and producers.
- Awards and recognition.

Wine tourism in Sardinia:

- Island attractions: landscapes, culture, gastronomy.
- Wine tourism itineraries and experiences.
- Wine-related events and festivals.
- The importance of wine tourism for the local economy.

Challenges and Perspectives:

- Production challenges in Sardinia: climate change, competition, market.
- Sustainability and environmental preservation.
- Research and innovation in viticulture.
- The future of winemaking in Sardinia.

Sardinia: The Wine Island with a Mediterranean Soul and Unique Character

Sardinia, the second largest island in the Mediterranean, is a paradise of wild beauty and ancient culture. While its paradisiacal beaches and archaeological sites attract attention from around the world, a treasure hides in its hills and plains: a rich winemaking tradition that produces wines with a unique and unmistakable character.

With a history that is intertwined with ancient Mediterranean civilizations, Sardinia has been cultivating vines for millennia, developing its own identity that is expressed in its wines. In this dive into Sardinian winemaking, we will explore the historical context of production on the island, uncover the geographical and climatic characteristics that shape its terroir and unveil the panorama of production, with its grapes, its wines and the challenges and potential that Sardinia faces on the world wine scene.

An Ancestral Legacy: The History of Wine in Sardinia and Italy

The history of wine in Sardinia is lost in the mists of time. Archaeological remains indicate that the vine was cultivated on the island more than 3,000 years ago, by the ancient Nuragic people. The Phoenicians, Carthaginians and Romans left their mark on Sardinian viticulture, introducing new varieties and cultivation techniques. Over the centuries, the island was conquered by different people, each leaving their contribution to the wine culture in the region. Byzantines, Arabs, Spanish and Piedmontese brought new grape varieties, winemaking techniques and wine styles, further enriching Sardinia's wine heritage.

Wine production in Sardinia has always been linked to the island's culture and everyday life. Wine was an essential element in food, festivities and religious rituals. Over the centuries, Sardinian viticulture has developed in harmony with the environment, adapting to the island's climatic conditions and soils. Traditional Sardinian winemaking practices have been passed down from generation to generation, preserving ancestral knowledge and ensuring continuity of production.

In the context of Italian viticulture, Sardinia occupies a special place. While other regions of Italy stand out for producing famous and renowned wines, Sardinia has preserved its identity and tradition, cultivating indigenous grape varieties and producing wines with unique characteristics, which reflect the island character and the richness of its terroir.

Sardinian Terroir: The Force of Nature in Wine

Sardinia's terroir is one of the key elements for the production of unique and expressive wines. The island has a diverse geography, with mountains, plains, hills and coasts that alternate, creating a variety of microclimates and soils. The Mediterranean climate, with hot, dry summers and mild, rainy winters, is ideal for growing vines. The influence of the sea, with its breezes and salt spray, also plays an important role in the formation of Sardinian terroir.

Sardinia's soils are equally diverse, ranging from sandy to clayey, from limestone to granite. This diversity of soils, combined with climatic and geographic variations, creates an infinite number of terroirs, each with its own characteristics and potential. The grapes grown in these different terroirs express in their wines the strength of nature and the uniqueness of Sardinia.

Wine Production in Sardinia: Grapes, Wines and Challenges

Sardinia has a wide variety of indigenous grapes, which represent a unique genetic heritage of great value for winemaking. Some of the main red grape varieties on the island are Cannonau, Carignano, Monica, Bovale Sardo and Muristellu. Enter the branch grapes, including Vermentino, Nuragus, Nasco, Semidano and Vernaccia di Oristano. These grapes, adapted to the Sardinian terroir, produce wines with distinctive characteristics that express the island's identity.

Sardinian wines are known for their intensity, complexity and elegance. The reds, made mainly with the Cannonau grape, are full-bodied, with aromas of ripe red fruits, spices and earthy notes. The whites, especially Vermentino, are fresh, aromatic and with good acidity. The island also produces sweet wines, such as Moscato di Sorso-Sennori and Vernaccia di Oristano, and sparkling wines, such as Vermentino Spumante.

Sardinian winemaking faces several challenges, such as competition from other producing regions, the need for modernization and the search for international markets. However, the island also has great potential, thanks to the quality of its wines, the diversity of its terroirs and the growing demand for authentic products with identity.

The Influence of the Mediterranean: Climate, Winds and Soils in Sardinian Viticulture

The Mediterranean climate, characteristic of Sardinia, is a determining factor in the island's viticulture. With hot, dry summers and mild winters, it provides ideal conditions for growing high-quality grapes. Generous sun exposure and the scarcity of rain during the grapes' maturation phase are crucial for the concentration of sugars and phenolic development, resulting in wines with remarkable structure, aromatic intensity and balance between acidity and sweetness.

The winds that blow over the island, such as the Mistral and Sirocco, play a fundamental role in Sardinian viticulture. The Mistral, a dry, cold wind that blows from the northwest, helps control humidity in the vineyards, reducing the risk of fungal diseases and contributing to the health of the grapes. Sirocco, a hot and dry wind coming from the south, can increase the temperature in the vineyards, accelerating the grape maturation process and intensifying the sugar concentration.

The diversity of soils in Sardinia is another factor that contributes to the richness and complexity of the island's wines. Granitic, limestone, clayey and sandy soils are present in different regions, giving unique characteristics to the wines produced in each area. Granitic soils, for example, tend to produce wines with good acidity and minerality, while calcareous soils can result in wines with greater body and structure. The presence of minerals in the soil, such as iron and granite, can also be perceived in the wines, adding layers of complexity and mineral nuances to their sensory profile.

Furthermore, the island's topography, with its hills and mountains, also influences viticulture. The different altitudes and solar exposure provide different microclimates, allowing the cultivation of a wide variety of grapes and the production of wines with different aromatic and taste profiles. The combination of these factors – climate, wind, soil and topography – creates a unique terroir in Sardinia, which is reflected in the quality and diversity of the wines produced on the island.

Production Overview: Grapes, Wines and Challenges in Sardinia

Sardinia, with its unique terroir and rich winemaking history, grows a wide variety of grapes, both native and international, which give rise to a diverse range of wines.

Red Grapes

- Cannonau: The island's most emblematic red grape, Cannonau, is the basis for full-bodied and complex red wines. With intense aromas of ripe red fruits, such as cherry and blackberry, complemented by spicy notes, such as black pepper and cloves, and a characteristic herbaceous touch, these wines have soft tannins and a long, persistent finish. Cannonau is a versatile grape, which can produce wines to be enjoyed young or with great aging potential.
- Carignano: Originally from Spain, Carignano found an ideal

terroir in Sardinia to express its potential. Its red wines are intense and structured, with aromas of ripe black fruits, such as plum and cassis, notes of spice and a mineral touch that reflects the island's soil. With firm tannins and good acidity, Sardinian Carignano wines have excellent aging potential, evolving in complexity and elegance over the years.

- Monica: A grape native to Sardinia, Monica yields light and fruity red wines, with aromas of fresh red fruits, such as strawberries and raspberries, and delicate floral notes. These are fresh, easy-drinking wines, ideal to accompany your day to day or to be enjoyed in relaxed moments.

White Grapes

- Vermentino: The most cultivated white grape in Sardinia, Vermentino, is the basis for aromatic and elegant white wines. With intense aromas of citrus fruits, such as lemon and grapefruit, white flowers and a mineral touch characteristic of the island's terroir, these wines are fresh, vibrant and gastronomic, combining perfectly with local cuisine based on seafood and pasta.

- Nuragus: A grape native to Sardinia, Nuragus yields light and refreshing white wines, with aromas of citrus fruits, such as lemon and lime, and notes of green apple. These are young and relaxed wines, ideal to be enjoyed on hot days or to accompany snacks and salads.

Diversity and Tradition

The diversity of grapes grown in Sardinia allows the production of a wide range of wines, from full-bodied and complex reds to light and refreshing whites, including rosés, sparkling wines and sweet wines. The island also stands out for producing wines using traditional methods, such as Vernaccia di Oristano, a white wine aged in oak barrels for long periods, which acquires complexity and unique aromas.

Challenges and Opportunities

Viticulture in Sardinia faces challenges such as water scarcity, soil erosion and competition from other producing regions. However, the island has enormous potential for the growth of its wine industry. The quality of its wines, the diversity of its terroir, the growing interest in wine tourism and investment in technology and sustainability are factors that drive the development of Sardinian viticulture.

Future Perspectives

With a long history, a unique terroir and a wide variety of grapes and wines, Sardinia has established itself as a wine region of great importance in Italy and the world. Its wines, which express the essence of the island and the passion of its producers, are winning over more and more connoisseurs in search of authenticity and a unique sensorial experience. Sardinia is becoming an increasingly sought-after destination for wine lovers, who want to explore its vineyards, meet its producers and taste its unique wines, which reflect the island's history, culture and natural beauty.

Sardinia: An Ancient Wine Odyssey in the Heart of the Mediterranean

Sardinia, an island of wild beauty and rich history nestled in the Mediterranean Sea, cultivates a winemaking tradition that dates back millennia. The sunny slopes, the Mediterranean climate and the influence of different cultures have shaped a unique terroir, where wines with a distinct character and striking personality are born. In this dive into the history of viticulture in Sardinia, we will uncover the origins of grape cultivation on the island, the traditions and customs related to wine, the evolution of production over the centuries and the fusion between tradition and innovation in modern Sardinian viticulture.

Origins of Viticulture: A Millennial Legacy

The history of viticulture in Sardinia is intertwined with the island's own history, marked by the influence of different peoples who sailed the Mediterranean waters. Archaeological evidence indicates that vine cultivation in Sardinia dates back more than 3,000 years, with the discovery of Vitis vinifera grape seeds in archaeological sites from the Nuragic era.

Phoenicians: It is believed that the Phoenicians, a trading and sailing people who established colonies in Sardinia around the 8th century BC, introduced new grape varieties and more advanced cultivation techniques, boosting wine production on the island. Their experience in maritime trade may also have facilitated the export of Sardinian wine to other Mediterranean regions, expanding their reach and influence.

Romans: From the 3rd century BC, the Romans conquered Sardinia and intensified wine production, which was exported to Rome and other regions of the Empire. The Romans introduced new winemaking techniques, such as the use of amphorae to transport and store wine, and built infrastructure, such as presses and cellars, which contributed to the development of viticulture on the island. Under Roman rule, Sardinia became an important wine production center, supplying the legions and the general population.

Other people: Over the centuries, Sardinia was dominated by different peoples, such as the Byzantines, the Arabs, the Spanish and the Italians. Each culture left its mark on Sardinian viticulture, introducing new grape varieties, growing techniques and wine styles. The Byzantine influence, for example, can be seen in the architecture of some wineries and the introduction of specific varieties. Spanish domination brought with it the tradition of producing fortified wines, while the Italian period contributed to the modernization of viticulture on the island.

Traditions and Customs: Wine and Culture

Wine has always been present in Sardinian culture, associated with festivals, religious rituals and people's daily lives. Traditions and customs related to wine reflect the importance of this drink in the history and identity of the Sardinian people.

Festivals and celebrations: Wine is an essential element in Sardinian festivals and celebrations, such as weddings, baptisms and religious festivals. In many festivals, wine is produced by hand by the families themselves, following recipes and traditions passed down from generation to generation. Each occasion has its own customs and rituals associated with wine, which symbolizes the joy, unity and hospitality of the Sardinian people.

Religious rituals: Wine is also present in religious rituals, such as Catholic mass, where it symbolizes the blood of Christ. In some regions of Sardinia, wine is used in pagan rituals of ancient origin, as offerings to nature deities. Wine, in this context, represents the connection between man and the divine, and is used to celebrate life, fertility and abundance.

Wine in everyday life: Wine is part of the everyday life of Sardinians, being consumed at meals and in moments of social interaction. It is common for families to produce their own wine for home consumption, keeping the tradition of family viticulture alive. Wine, in Sardinia, is not just a drink, but an element that unites people, strengthens family ties and celebrates community life.

Production Evolution: Challenges and Achievements

Wine production in Sardinia has evolved over the centuries, facing challenges and gaining recognition for the quality and typicality of its wines.

Challenges: Sardinian viticulture has faced several challenges throughout history. Pests and diseases, such as the phylloxera that devastated European vineyards in the late 19th century, required replanting and adaptation to new conditions. Furthermore, wars and economic crises impacted production and trade, leading to periods of stagnation and difficulties in maintaining vineyards and wine production. Water scarcity and climate change, with periods of drought and extreme temperatures, also represent challenges for Sardinian viticulture, requiring the adoption of sustainable practices and the search for more resistant grape varieties.

Achievements: Despite the challenges, Sardinian viticulture has gained recognition for the quality and typicality of its wines. The creation of designations of origin (DOCs), starting in the 1970s, was fundamental to protect and enhance the island's wines, establishing strict rules for production and guaranteeing the authenticity and quality of the wines. Wines such as Cannonau, Vermentino and Carignano del Sulcis have gained international fame, consolidating Sardinia as a region producing excellent wines, attracting investment, tourism and recognition in demanding markets. Participation in international fairs and competitions also contributed to the dissemination and appreciation of Sardinian wines, winning awards and recognition from specialized critics.

Influence of Cultures: A Mosaic of Flavors

Sardinian viticulture has been influenced by diverse cultures and dominations throughout history, creating a mosaic of grape varieties, growing techniques and wine styles.

Spanish influence: During the period of Spanish domination, new grape varieties were introduced to Sardinia, such as Cannonau (Grenache) and Carignano. The Spanish influence is also reflected in some winemaking techniques, such as aging in oak barrels, and in the styles of wine produced, with an emphasis on full-bodied wines with good storage capacity.

French influence: French influence was felt in Sardinia from the 18th century onwards, with the introduction of varieties such as Vermentino and Cabernet Sauvignon. The French also contributed to the modernization of viticulture on the island, with the introduction of new cultivation and winemaking techniques.

Italian influence: The unification of Italy in the 19th century brought greater integration of Sardinia with the rest of the country. Sardinian viticulture has benefited from the exchange of knowledge and technologies with other Italian regions, as well as having access to a wider and more diverse consumer market.

Tradition and Innovation: Modern Sardinia

Wine production in modern Sardinia combines tradition and innovation, seeking to preserve the identity and typicality of the wines, while incorporating new technologies and knowledge.

Preservation of traditions: Many Sardinian producers keep winemaking traditions alive, cultivating indigenous grape varieties, using traditional cultivation methods and producing wines in the region's classic style. This approach values the history and culture of Sardinian viticulture, keeping the connection with the past alive and preserving the uniqueness of the island's wines.

Technological innovation: At the same time, Sardinian viticulture benefits from technological innovation, with the introduction of new cultivation techniques, such as temperature control in fermentation and the use of selected yeasts, and winemaking, such as carbonic maceration and the use of oak barrels of different origins. These innovations make it possible to improve the quality of wines, increase production efficiency and create new styles of wine, meeting market demands and consumer expectations.

Sustainability: Environmental sustainability is a growing concern in Sardinian viticulture. Many producers adopt sustainable practices, such as the use of renewable energy, reducing the use of pesticides and implementing more efficient irrigation systems. These practices aim to minimize the environmental impact of viticulture, preserve natural resources and ensure the longevity of the activity.

Sardinia, with its rich history and winemaking tradition, has established itself as a region producing unique and authentic wines. The combination of natural factors, such as the Mediterranean climate, volcanic soils and the influence of the sea, with cultural influences and the passion of producers results in wines that express the soul of the island, conquering palates around the world and standing out on the international wine scene.

Sardinian Terroir: The Essence of the Island Reflected in its Wines

Sardinia, the second largest island in the Mediterranean, is a paradise of natural beauty and rich history, where viticulture has played a fundamental role for millennia. Sardinian terroir, a unique combination of natural and human factors, gives the island's wines a distinct identity and fascinating complexity. In this deep dive into Sardinian terroir, we will explore the influence of the Mediterranean climate, the diversity of soils and microclimates, wine regions and their contribution to the typicality of Sardinian wines.

The Embrace of the Mediterranean: Sun, Wind and Thermal Range

Sardinia is bathed by the Mediterranean Sea, which has a marked influence on the island's climate. The Mediterranean climate, with hot, dry summers and mild, rainy winters, is ideal for growing vines. The abundance of sun favors photosynthesis and the accumulation of sugars in the grapes, while the temperature range between day and night contributes to the preservation of acidity and aromas, resulting in balanced and complex wines.

Winds, such as the Mistral and Sirocco, also play an important role in the Sardinian terroir. The Mistral, a cool, dry wind that blows from the northwest, helps regulate humidity and reduce the risk of fungal diseases in vines. The Sirocco, a hot and humid wind that blows from the south, can bring with it sand from the Sahara desert, which is deposited in the island's soil and contributes to its minerality. These winds also help to concentrate the aromas in the grapes, resulting in wines with greater aromatic intensity.

Soils and Microclimates: A Mosaic of Diversity

Sardinia has a great diversity of soils, a result of its complex geological history. The island has sandy, clayey, limestone, granite and volcanic soils, each with its own characteristics and contributions to the wines. Sandy soils, for example, are well drained and tend to produce lighter, fruitier wines. Clay soils retain more moisture and nutrients, resulting in fuller-bodied wines with more present tannins. Limestone soils, in turn, contribute to the minerality and acidity of wines, while granite and volcanic soils provide mineral and spicy notes.

The island's rugged topography, with mountains, hills and plains, creates a multitude of microclimates. Variations in altitude, sun exposure and proximity to the sea influence the ripening of the grapes and give specific characteristics to the wines from each location. For example, vineyards located at higher altitudes tend to have lower temperatures and greater thermal amplitude, which favors the production of wines with greater acidity and freshness. Vineyards located close to the sea are influenced by sea breezes, which help regulate temperature and humidity, resulting in wines with unique characteristics.

Wine Regions and Typicality of Sardinian Wines

Sardinia has several wine-growing regions, each with its own characteristics and varieties of grapes grown. Some of the main regions include:

- **Campidano of Cagliari:** Located in the south of the island, this region is known for its full-bodied red wines, produced from grapes such as Cannonau, Carignano and Monica.
- **Logudoro:** Located in the northwest of Sardinia, this region produces high quality red and white wines, from grapes such

as Vermentino, Cannonau and Cagnulari.

- **Gallura:** Located in the northeast of the island, this region is famous for its fresh, aromatic white wines, produced from the Vermentino grape.
- **Alghero:** Located in the northwest of Sardinia, this region produces high quality red and white wines, from grapes such as Vermentino, Cannonau and Torbato.

The typicality of Sardinian wines is the result of the interaction between all these factors - climate, soil, topography, grape varieties and winemaking practices. Sardinian wines are known for their aromatic intensity, complexity and aging capacity. They are an authentic expression of Sardinian terroir and a testament to the island's rich wine heritage.

Sardinia Wine Regions: A Deep Dive into the Wine Island

Sardinia, an island bathed in sunshine and the Mediterranean Sea, is a hidden treasure for wine lovers. With a rich wine-growing history dating back millennia, the island has several wine-producing regions, each with its distinct characteristics and unique traditions.

Gallura: O Reino do Vermentino

In the northeast of the island, the Gallura region is a paradise for white wine lovers. The Vermentino grape, star of the region, finds the perfect terroir here to express its full potential. The Mediterranean climate, softened by the sea breeze, and the granite soils, rich in minerals, give Gallura wines a unique personality: citrus and herbaceous aromas, subtle mineral notes and a vibrant acidity that invites you to the next sip.

Trexenta: Ashore from Monica

In southern Sardinia, the Trexenta region is known for its intense, full-bodied red wines. The Monica grape, a variety native to the island, finds its home here. The hot and dry climate, combined with clayey soils, gives rise to wines with soft, silky tannins, aromas of ripe red fruits and a touch of spice that adds complexity and elegance.

Mandrolisai: The Birthplace of Cannonau

In the heart of Sardinia, the Mandrolisai region is the birthplace of Cannonau, the island's most emblematic red grape. The continental climate, with hot days and cool nights, and the limestone soils, rich in minerals, are the ideal setting for the production of red wines with structure, firm tannins and intense aromas of black fruits and spices. Mandrolisai wines are known for their ability to age, evolving in the bottle for many years and revealing new layers of complexity over time.

Alghero: The Catalan Influence

On the west coast of the island, the Alghero region is a testament to Sardinia's rich history and cultural influences. With a strong presence of Catalan culture, the region is known for its red and white wines that reflect this heritage. The Cabernet Sauvignon grape, originally from Bordeaux, finds here an exceptional terroir to produce full-bodied and complex red wines, with aromas of black fruits, spices and notes of cedar. The Torbato grape, a variety native to Sardinia, gives rise to aromatic and mineral white wines, with citrus and floral notes and a long, persistent finish.

Typical: The Soul of Sardinian Wines

Typicality is what defines Sardinian wines. It is the ability of each wine to express its origin, its terroir, in each aroma, in each flavor. It's the minerality of the soils, the freshness of the Mediterranean climate, the intensity of the native grapes. It is the history and culture of the island, translated into every drop of wine.

Sardinian wines are an invitation to a sensory journey around the island, a unique experience that awakens the senses and thrills the palate. In each glass, discover the essence of Sardinia, its soul, its history.

Sardinian Grapes: A Treasure of Biodiversity and Tradition in

the Mediterranean

Sardinia, an Italian island of wild beauty and ancient culture, is a paradise for viticulture. With a rich heritage of indigenous grapes that produce wines of unique and expressive character, the island, isolated in the heart of the Mediterranean, has preserved an invaluable genetic heritage, with more than 120 varieties of native grapes, many of them practically unknown in other parts of the world.

Indigenous Varieties: The Soul of Sardinian Winemaking

Paints:

- **Cannonau:** The most planted red grape in Sardinia, Cannonau (synonymous with Grenache), produces full-bodied red wines, with intense aromas of ripe red fruits, spices and herbaceous notes. Its wines are known for their tannic structure, balanced acidity and good aging potential. Cannonau stands out in the production of high quality red wines, especially in the controlled designations of origin (DOC) Cannonau di Sardegna and Nepente di Oliena. This grape adapts well to the island's poor, stony soils and hot, dry climate, resulting in wines with a high alcohol content and firm tannins.
- **Carignano:** A grape of Spanish origin, Carignano found an ideal terroir in Sardinia to express its strength and rusticity. Its red wines are full-bodied, with robust tannins, high acidity and aromas of ripe black fruits, spices and earthy notes. Carignano is grown mainly in the south of the island, in the Sulcis region, where it produces wines of great character and longevity. Due to their high acidity and tannins, Carignano wines are often aged in oak to soften their structure and add complexity.
- **Monica:** A traditional Sardinian red grape, Monica produces light to medium red wines, with fruity aromas, soft tannins and moderate acidity. Their wines are easy to drink, with notes of fresh red fruits, spices and an herbaceous touch. Monica is grown in several areas of the island, being used for

both varietal wines and blends. It is a versatile grape that can be vinified in various styles, from young and fruity wines to fuller-bodied and aged wines.

- **Bovale Sardo:** A red grape native to Sardinia, Bovale Sardo produces full-bodied red wines, with robust tannins, high acidity and aromas of ripe black fruits, spices and notes of licorice. Its wines are known for their structure and aging potential. Bovale Sardo is cultivated mainly in the Sulcis region, where it contributes to the production of red wines of great character. This grape is drought resistant and adapts well to the hot, sunny conditions of Sardinia.

- **Tour:** Rare and ancient red grape, cultivated mainly in the Cagliari region, in the south of Sardinia. Girò produces light to medium red wines, with delicate aromas of red fruits, spices and floral notes. Its wines are fresh, with soft tannins and balanced acidity. Girò is a variety that represents the richness and diversity of Sardinia's genetic heritage. Due to their rarity and limited production, Girò wines are difficult to find outside of Sardinia.

White:

- **Vermentino:** The most important white grape in Sardinia, Vermentino produces aromatic white wines, with notes of citrus fruits, white flowers and a mineral touch. Its wines are known for their freshness, vibrant acidity and elegance. Vermentino is grown in several areas of the island, with emphasis on the Gallura region, in the north, where it produces high quality wines. This grape adapts well to Gallura's granite and sandy soils, resulting in wines with distinct minerality and refreshing acidity.

- **Nuragus:** A traditional white grape from Sardinia, Nuragus produces light and refreshing white wines, with delicate aromas of citrus fruits, white flowers and an herbaceous touch. Its wines are easy to drink, with moderate acidity and a pleasant finish. Nuragus is cultivated throughout the island, being one of the oldest varieties in Sardinia. It is a high-yielding and resistant grape, but with the potential to produce quality wines when the grapes are harvested at the right time and vinified with care.

- **Vernaccia di Oristano:** A white grape grown exclusively in the Oristano region of Sardinia, Vernaccia di Oristano produces unique white wines, with complex aromas of dried fruits, honey, spices and oxidative notes. Its wines are full-bodied, with high acidity and great aging potential. Vernaccia di Oristano is one of the oldest grapes in Italy, with a tradition dating back centuries. The production of Vernaccia di Oristano involves a unique oxidative aging process, which gives the wines their distinctive character.

Other Varieties Grown in Sardinia

In addition to indigenous varieties, Sardinia successfully grows other grapes, both Italian and international, which have adapted well to the island's climate and soil and contribute to the diversity and richness of its wine panorama. Among the international red varieties, Cabernet Sauvignon stands out, with its firm tannins and aromas of black fruits, and Merlot, which gives softness and elegance to the wines. Syrah, with its notes of spice and pepper, and Sangiovese, an emblematic Tuscan grape that adds structure and acidity, also find favorable conditions in Sardinia for the production of high quality wines.

Among the white varieties, Chardonnay, with its versatility and ability to express terroir, and Sauvignon Blanc, with its citrus and herbaceous aromas, stand out in the production of aromatic and refreshing white wines. Moscato, with its natural sweetness and floral aromas, is widely used in the production of sweet and sparkling wines.

Preservation of Biodiversity and Sustainability

The preservation of Sardinia's native varieties is of paramount importance to maintain the island's biodiversity, history and cultural identity. Many of these varieties, which represent a unique genetic heritage, are threatened with extinction due to competition with international varieties, the loss of old vineyards and climate change.

Fortunately, there is a growing interest in preserving and promoting these unique grapes. Many producers are adopting sustainable and organic practices, such as using natural fertilizers, reducing the use of pesticides and implementing growing techniques that respect the environment. Furthermore, they are rescuing old vineyards and promoting research and development of winemaking techniques that value the unique characteristics of native grapes.

Preservation of Native Grapes: A Legacy for the Future

The preservation of Sardinia's native grapes is a legacy for future generations. These varieties, which have adapted to the Sardinian terroir over centuries, represent a unique genetic heritage and offer invaluable oenological potential. The production of wines with native grapes contributes to the appreciation of local culture, the diversification of the wine supply, the development of wine tourism and the sustainability of viticulture on the island.

Other Varieties: Enriching the Wine Mosaic

In addition to indigenous varieties, Sardinia grows other grapes, both Italian and international, which contribute to the diversity and richness of its wine scene. Among the reds, Sangiovese stands out, with its structure and acidity, Merlot, with its softness and elegance, and Cabernet Sauvignon, with its firm tannins and aromas of black fruits. Among the whites, Malvasia, with its floral and fruity aromas, Nasco, with its acidity and aging potential, and Semidano, with its versatility and ability to express the terroir, are widely cultivated on the island. These varieties, combined with native grapes, allow the production of a wide range of wines, which express the diversity of the Sardinian terroir and the creativity of its producers.

In short, Sardinian grapes represent a treasure of biodiversity, history and tradition, which gives the island a prominent place on the world wine scene. The preservation of native varieties, the exploration of their oenological potential and the combination with other grapes guarantee the richness, uniqueness and diversity of Sardinian wines, which are gaining more and more connoisseurs around the globe.

The Art of Winemaking in Sardinia: Tradition and Innovation in Search of Terroir Expression

Sardinia, an Italian island of wild beauty and rich culture, has an ancient winemaking tradition that is intertwined with its history and identity. From ancient cultivation techniques to modern winemaking methods, Sardinian producers seek to express the essence of terroir — the set of unique characteristics of soil, climate and topography of a given region — in each bottle, creating wines with typicality and personality. In this dive into the world of wine production in Sardinia, we will explore vineyard management, winemaking techniques, the creation of different styles of wine and the fundamental role of the winemaker in expressing Sardinian terroir.

Vineyard Management: Adapting to Climate and Soil

Sardinia's Mediterranean climate, with hot, dry summers and mild winters, directly influences vine cultivation. Sardinian producers have developed, over the centuries, vineyard management techniques adapted to the island's climatic conditions and soil types. One of the main challenges facing Sardinian winegrowers is water scarcity, especially during the summer months. To overcome this problem, several strategies are adopted, such as planting vines on slopes, where rainwater drains naturally, and the use of drip irrigation systems, which allow for more efficient use of water.

Climate adaptation: To deal with summer heat and drought, winegrowers use techniques such as green pruning, which reduces foliage and allows better air circulation between vines, and choosing drought-resistant rootstocks. The rootstock is the part of the vine that is buried in the soil and provides support and nutrients to the plant. Choosing the correct rootstock is essential for the vine's adaptation to the climate and soil. In some areas, precision irrigation is used to supplement the water needs of plants.

Solo Types: Sardinia has a great diversity of soils, from the sandy and granitic soils of the coastal areas to the clayey and limestone soils of the interior. Producers choose the most suitable grape varieties for each type of soil, seeking the best balance between the plant and the terroir. For example, sandy soils are ideal for growing white grapes, while clayey soils are more suitable for red grapes.

Winemaking Techniques: Tradition and Modernity

Sardinia preserves a rich tradition in wine production, with ancestral methods passed down from generation to generation. However, producers are also open to innovation, incorporating modern technologies to improve the quality and typicity of wines.

Traditional methods: Fermentation in cement tanks or large wooden vessels, aging in oak barrels and the use of indigenous yeasts are some of the traditional methods that are still used in Sardinia. These techniques contribute to the complexity and expression of terroir in wines. Indigenous yeasts, for example, are microorganisms that are naturally present on grapes and in the winery environment and that give unique characteristics to wines.

Modern methods: Temperature control during fermentation, micro oxygenation and the use of clarification and filtration techniques are some examples of modern methods that have been incorporated into winemaking in Sardinia. These technologies allow winemakers greater control over the production process, resulting in wines with greater precision and quality. Micro oxygenation, for example, is a technique that consists of adding small amounts of oxygen to wine during aging, which contributes to stabilizing color and aromas.

Different Wine Styles: A Palette of Flavors in Sardinia

The rich diversity of grape varieties, the influence of diverse terroirs and the different winemaking techniques employed by Sardinian producers result in a wide and fascinating range of wine styles. Each wine tells a unique story, expressing the essence of the land and the passion of the winegrowers.

Red Wines: Red wines are the most produced in Sardinia, representing the soul and tradition of the island. Made with grapes such as Cannonau, Monica, Carignano and Bovale, each variety contributes unique characteristics to the final wine. Sardinian reds are known for their robust structure, striking tannins that provide a sensation of astringency in the mouth, and intense aromas of ripe red and black fruits, such as cherry, blackberry and plum. Complementing the aromatic profile are notes of spices, such as black pepper and cloves, and herbaceous nuances, reminiscent of Mediterranean herbs, such as rosemary and thyme.

- **Cannonau:** The most emblematic grape of Sardinia, it produces full-bodied wines, with a high alcohol content and aromas of ripe black fruits, spices and earthy notes.
- **Monica:** Red grape that gives rise to medium-bodied wines, with soft tannins, aromas of red fruits and floral notes.
- **Carignano:** Variety that produces wines with good structure, firm tannins and aromas of black fruits, spices and balsamic notes.
- **Bovale:** Grape that contributes to full-bodied wines, with intense tannins and aromas of ripe black fruits and spices.

White Wines: Sardinian white wines offer a refreshing and vibrant experience, perfect for the island's sunny days. Made with grapes such as Vermentino, Nuragus and Vernaccia, these wines stand out for their balanced acidity, which provides a sensation of freshness in the mouth, and for the delicate aromas of citrus fruits, such as lemon and grapefruit, and white flowers, such as jasmine and orange blossom.

- **Vermentino:** The most cultivated white grape in Sardinia, it produces wines with good acidity, citrus and floral aromas, and a mineral touch.
- **Nuragus:** Native grape that gives rise to light and fresh wines, with citrus and floral aromas.
- **Vernaccia:** Variety that produces wines with good structure, balanced acidity and aromas of tropical fruits and almond notes.

Rosé Wines: Sardinian rosé wines enchant with their beauty and delicacy. Produced mainly with the Cannonau grape, but also with other red varieties, such as Monica and Grenache, these wines have a soft and bright pink color, intense aromas of fresh red fruits, such as strawberry and raspberry, and a light, refreshing and fruity palate.

Sparkling wines: Sardinia also stands out in the production of high-quality sparkling wines, made both by the traditional method, with the second fermentation in the bottle, and by the Charmat method, with the second fermentation in stainless steel tanks. Sardinian sparkling wines surprise with their creaminess, the result of fine and persistent bubbles, their balanced acidity, which contributes to the sensation of freshness, and their fruity and floral aromas, which vary according to the grapes used and the maturation time.

Fortified Wines: Sardinia's winemaking tradition is also expressed in fortified wines, such as Vernaccia di Oristano, a unique liqueur wine, produced from the Vernaccia grape. The fortification process, which consists of adding wine alcohol during fermentation, gives the wine greater alcohol content and sweetness. Vernaccia di Oristano is aged for long periods in oak barrels, acquiring aromatic complexity, with notes of dried fruits, honey, caramel and spices, and an intense, persistent and velvety taste.

A Sensory Experience:

The diversity of Sardinian wine styles invites you to a unique sensory journey, exploring aromas, flavors and textures that reflect the richness of the land and the island's winemaking tradition. Each sip is an invitation to discover the essence of Sardinia, in an experience that delights the senses and celebrates the passion for wine.

The Search for Identity and Typicality: Valuing the Sardinian Terroir

Sardinian producers are increasingly aware of the importance of expressing the identity and typicality of the terroir in their wines. The appreciation of indigenous grape varieties, such as Cannonau, Vermentino and Nuragus, and the search for cultivation and winemaking practices that respect the environment and tradition contribute to the creation of wines with a unique and recognizable character.

The Winemaker: Artist and Interpreter of Terroir

The winemaker plays a fundamental role in expressing terroir in Sardinian wines. He is responsible for interpreting the characteristics of the soil, climate and grapes, and for conducting the winemaking process in order to extract the best from each variety and each vineyard.

The Sardinian winemaker needs to have a deep knowledge of the island's terroir, grape varieties and winemaking techniques. He must be able to make decisions that respect tradition, but that also incorporate innovations that improve the quality and typicality of the wines.

In short, wine production in Sardinia is an art that combines tradition, innovation and a deep respect for the terroir. Sardinian producers are dedicated to creating wines that express the essence of the island, with their own identity and a striking personality. When you taste a Sardinian wine, you are experiencing not just a drink, but also the history, culture and soul of this Mediterranean island.

Appellations of Origin in Sardinia: A Deep Dive into the Quality and Tradition of Italian Wines

Italy, with its rich and long history of wine production, has a rigorous classification system to ensure the quality and authenticity of its wines. Denominations of Origin, made up of the categories DOCG (Denominazione di Origine Controllata e Garantita), DOC (Denominazione di Origine Controllata) and IGT (Indicazione Geografica Tipica), function as a seal of quality, guaranteeing consumers the geographic origin and typicality of the wines. Sardinia, an island of wild beauty and ancient traditions, has a unique wine heritage, with denominations of origin that reflect the diversity of its terroir and the richness of its grape varieties. In this deep dive into Sardinia's appellations of origin, we will explore: the Italian classification system, the island's main appellations, their regulations and specificities, and the production of table wines outside the appellations.

The Italian Classification System: DOCG, DOC and IGT

The Italian wine classification system is based on three main categories:

- **DOCG (Controlled and Guaranteed Designation of Origin):** The most prestigious category, which designates high quality wines produced in defined geographical areas, with strict production and quality control rules. DOCG wines undergo sensory and chemical analyzes to ensure they comply with the denomination's standards and must be bottled in the production region itself.
- **DOC (Controlled Designation of Origin):** Intermediate category, which designates wines produced in specific geographic areas, with production rules defined to guarantee typicality and quality. DOC wines must follow standards regarding permitted grape varieties, cultivation methods and winemaking techniques.
- **IGT (Typical Geographical Indication):** Broader and

more flexible category, which designates wines produced in a specific geographic region. IGT wines allow the use of a greater variety of grapes and winemaking methods, but are required to display the grape variety on the label.

Main Appellations of Origin in Sardinia

Sardinia, an island of exuberant natural beauty and ancient traditions, has a unique and diverse wine heritage. The island's designations of origin reflect the diversity of its terroir and the richness of its grape varieties, giving rise to wines with identity and personality. Some of the main appellations in Sardinia are:

- **Vermentino di Gallura DOCG:** Produced in the Gallura region, in the north of the island, this appellation is famous for its white wines made with the Vermentino grape. Vermentino di Gallura DOCG wines are known for their aromas of citrus fruits, white flowers and mineral notes, in addition to their refreshing acidity and persistent finish.
- **Cannonau di Sardegna DOC:** One of the most important appellations on the island, which covers several sub-regions, Cannonau di Sardegna DOC produces red wines made with the Cannonau (Grenache) grape. Cannonau di Sardegna DOC wines are known for their aromas of ripe red fruits, spices and herbaceous notes, in addition to their tannic structure and good aging potential.
- **Carignano del Sulcis DOC:** Produced in the Sulcis region, in the south of the island, this appellation is known for its red wines made with the Carignano grape. Carignano del Sulcis DOC wines are full-bodied wines, with firm tannins, aromas of ripe black fruits, spices and mineral notes, and excellent aging potential.
- **Monica di Sardegna DOC:** This appellation covers the entire island and produces red wines made with the Monica grape. Monica di Sardegna DOC wines are light to medium wines, with soft tannins, aromas of fresh red fruits and an easy drinking character.
- **Nuragus di Cagliari DOC:** Produced in the Cagliari region, in the south of the island, this appellation is known

for its white wines made with the Nuragus grape. Nuragus di Cagliari DOC wines are light and refreshing wines, with aromas of citrus fruits and white flowers.

- **Vernaccia di Oristano DOC:** Produced in the Oristano region, in the west of the island, this appellation is famous for its white wines made with the Vernaccia grape. Vernaccia di Oristano DOC wines are complex and full-bodied wines, with aromas of dried fruits, honey and spices, and a long aging potential.

Denomination Regulations and Specifications

Each Sardinian designation of origin has its own rules and specifications, which define aspects such as:

- **Geographic production area:** Precise delimitation of the area where the grapes must be grown.
- **Allowed grape varieties:** Specification of the grape varieties that can be used in the production of wines and percentages of each one, when necessary.
- **Maximum yields:** Limitation of the quantity of grapes that can be harvested per hectare, to guarantee quality and concentration of flavors.
- **Cultivation methods:** Standards relating to vine training systems, pruning and permitted phytosanitary treatments.
- **Winemaking techniques:** Rules for making wines, such as the type of fermentation, the use of oak barrels and aging time.
- **Organoleptic characteristics:** Definition of the sensory characteristics that wines must present, such as color, aroma, flavor, alcohol content and structure.
- **Minimum aging:** Minimum aging time that the wine must have before being sold.
- **Labeling specifications:** Mandatory information that must appear on the wine label, such as the designation of origin, vintage and producer.

Table Wines and Sardinia: A Brief Approach

In addition to wines with designation of origin, Sardinia also produces table wines, which are not subject to DOCG, DOC and IGT regulations. These wines can be made with a greater variety of grapes and winemaking techniques, offering producers greater creative freedom. Although they do not have the same prestige as designations of origin, Sardinian table wines can be of high quality and represent an excellent option for consumers looking for wines with good value for money.

The Importance of Designations of Origin for Sardinia

Designations of origin play a fundamental role in protecting and enhancing Sardinia's wine heritage. They guarantee the quality and authenticity of the wines produced on the island, promoting its identity and reputation in the national and international market. Furthermore, designations of origin contribute to the economic and social development of Sardinia, encouraging oenological tourism and the preservation of the island's winemaking traditions.

Table Wines and Production "Outside" Denominations

Table wines, also known as "vini da tavola", are wines that do not fall into the DOCG, DOC or IGT categories. These wines can be produced with grapes from different regions, without restrictions on varieties or production methods.

Although table wines do not have the same reputation as wines with a designation of origin, Sardinia has a tradition of producing good quality homemade and artisanal wines. These wines, often made with indigenous grapes and traditional methods, represent an important part of the island's wine culture.

In recent years, there has been a growing interest in producing wines "outside" the appellations, with producers seeking to express the diversity of terroir and experiment with new winemaking techniques. These wines, although they do not have an official quality seal, can offer unique and surprising sensory experiences.

In conclusion, Sardinian designations of origin represent a valuable heritage of Italian viticulture, guaranteeing the quality, origin and typicality of the island's wines. By learning about the Italian classification system and the main Sardinian appellations, you will be able to appreciate the richness and diversity of Sardinian wines, enjoying an authentic and memorable wine and gastronomic experience.

The Wines of Sardinia: A Sensory Journey through the Island of Treasures

Sardinia, the second largest island in the Mediterranean, is a paradise of natural beauty and rich history, where wine culture is intertwined with Sardinian identity. Isolated from the mainland, the island has developed a unique winemaking tradition, with native grape varieties that give rise to wines with a distinct character and striking personality. In this deep dive into Sardinian wines, we will explore their sensory profiles, unveil the characteristics of each variety, harmonize with local cuisine and present the main producers and labels that elevate the island to the level of reference in the world of wine.

Sensory Profiles: Uncovering the Aromas and Flavors of Sardinia

Sardinian wines are a reflection of its unique terroir, marked by the Mediterranean climate, volcanic soils and the influence of the sea. The native varieties, cultivated for centuries on the island, give the wines their own identity and an aromatic complexity that differentiates them from other Italian wines.

Red Wines:

- **Cannonau:** The most planted red grape in Sardinia, Cannonau (Grenache) produces full-bodied red wines, with intense aromas of ripe red fruits, such as cherry, blackberry and plum, as well as spicy notes, such as black pepper and cloves. On the palate, they have soft tannins, good

31

acidity and a long, persistent finish. Quality Cannonaus have great aging potential, evolving in the bottle and developing complex aromas of leather, tobacco and cocoa, as well as earthy and coffee notes. They pair well with grilled or roasted red meat, pasta with rich sauces and aged cheeses.

- **Carignano del Sulcis:** Grown mainly in the southern region of the island, Carignano (Carignan) produces robust red wines, with a high concentration of tannins and high acidity. Its aromas are intense, with notes of black fruits, such as blackberries and blueberries, spices, licorice and a mineral touch characteristic of the region. With aging, Carignano del Sulcis wines soften their tannins and develop complex aromas of damp earth, leather and tobacco, gaining elegance and complexity. These are wines that call for equally intense dishes, such as game meats, stews and strong cheeses.

- **Monica:** A red grape native to Sardinia, Monica gives rise to light and fruity red wines, with aromas of fresh red fruits, such as strawberries and raspberries, and delicate floral notes. On the palate, they are soft wines, with soft tannins and balanced acidity. These are easy-drinking wines, ideal for young consumption and to accompany light dishes, such as pasta with fresh sauces, salads and grilled white meats.

- **Other red varieties:** Although less known, other red varieties indigenous to Sardinia, such as Bovale Sardo, Caddiu and Girò, also contribute to the diversity and richness of the island's red wines, each with its unique characteristics and specific aromas.

White Wines:

- **Vermentino di Gallura:** Vermentino di Gallura is one of Sardinia's most famous white wines. Produced in the northeast region of the island, it has intense aromas of citrus fruits, such as lemon and grapefruit, white flowers, such as acacia and jasmine, and a distinct mineral and saline touch, a result of the influence of the sea and the region's granite soils. On the palate, it is a fresh wine, with vibrant acidity, medium body and a persistent finish, with citrus and mineral notes. Pairs perfectly with seafood, grilled fish, risottos and salads.

- **Vernaccia di Oristano:** Produced in the western region of the island, Vernaccia di Oristano is a unique white wine, with oxidative characteristics that give it complexity and longevity. Its aromas are reminiscent of dried fruits, such as almonds and hazelnuts, honey, spices and oxidative notes reminiscent of walnuts and caramel, the result of the aging process in oak barrels. On the palate, it is a dry wine, with high acidity, medium body and a long, complex finish, with notes of dried fruits and spices. It is a wine to be enjoyed with equally complex dishes, such as aged cheeses, foie gras and honey-based desserts.

- **Nuragus:** A white grape native to Sardinia, Nuragus produces light and refreshing white wines, with aromas of citrus fruits, green apple and white flowers. On the palate, they are wines with moderate acidity, light body and a pleasant finish. These are versatile wines, ideal for young consumption and to accompany everyday dishes, such as pasta with simple sauces, salads, appetizers and light fish dishes.

- **Other white varieties:** Sardinia also has other native white varieties, such as Nasco, Semidano and Torbato, which produce wines with unique characteristics and aromas that reflect the island's terroir.

Sweet Wines:

- **Moscato di Sorso-Sennori:** Produced in the northwest region of the island, Moscato di Sorso-Sennori is a sweet wine with intense aromas of tropical fruits, such as pineapple and mango, honey, white flowers and a touch of spices. On the palate, it is a sweet wine, but with balanced acidity, which gives it freshness and elegance.

- **Malvasia di Bosa:** Grown in the western region of the island, Malvasia di Bosa produces sweet wines with aromas of dried fruits, such as apricot and fig, honey, spices and oxidative notes. On the palate, it is a sweet and full-bodied wine, with a good balance between sweetness and acidity.

Uncovering the Characteristics of Sardinian Wines

- **Full-Bodied Red Wines:** Cannonau and Carignano del Sulcis are the main grapes that give rise to Sardinia's full-bodied red wines. These wines are characterized by aromatic intensity, tannic structure, good acidity and excellent aging potential. These are wines that pair well with dishes rich in flavor, such as grilled red meat, game, cured cheeses and dishes with intense sauces.
- **Aromatic White Wines:** Vermentino di Gallura and Vernaccia di Oristano are the main representatives of Sardinian aromatic white wines. These wines stand out for their aromatic intensity and complexity, vibrant acidity and good structure. They pair well with dishes based on fish, seafood, pasta with light sauces, risottos, white meats and fresh cheeses.
- **Light and Fruity Wines:** Monica and Nuragus give rise to red and white wines, respectively, with a lighter and fruitier profile. These are easy-drinking wines, with soft tannins and moderate acidity, ideal for young consumption and to accompany everyday dishes, such as pasta with simple sauces, salads, appetizers, grilled fish and white meats.
- **Sweet Wines:** Moscato di Sorso-Sennori and Malvasia di Bosa are examples of sweet wines from Sardinia, with intense and complex aromas. They pair well with desserts, blue cheeses and dried fruits.

The Influence of Terroir:

Sardinia's Mediterranean climate, with hot, dry summers and mild winters, is ideal for growing high-quality grapes. The island's volcanic and granite soils give the wines a mineral and saline character, while the influence of the sea provides freshness and unique aromas.

The History of Viticulture in Sardinia:

Viticulture in Sardinia dates back to the time of the Phoenicians, who introduced the first vines to the island. Over the centuries, wine culture has developed and adapted to the Sardinian terroir, giving rise to autochthonous varieties and wines with unique characteristics.

Sardinia: A Paradise for Wine Lovers

With its rich history, unique terroir and indigenous varieties, Sardinia is an unmissable destination for wine lovers. The island offers a complete sensory experience, with wines that reflect its culture, history and natural beauty.

Pairing with Sardinian Gastronomy: An Explosion of Flavors

Sardinian cuisine, rich in flavors and traditions, with dishes that reflect the island's history and culture, offers a unique gastronomic experience. Pairing with local wines, produced in the different regions of Sardinia with native and international grapes, enhances the flavors and provides a true immersion in the island's culture, creating unforgettable moments at the table.

Pig: Roast suckling pig, one of Sardinia's most emblematic dishes, prepared slowly on a spit or in a wood-fired oven, pairs perfectly with full-bodied red wines, such as Cannonau, known for its soft tannins and aromas of ripe red fruits, and Carignano del Sulcis, with notes of spice and licorice that complement the flavor of the succulent meat. The tannic structure of the wine balances the fat of the suckling pig, while the fruity and spicy notes highlight the complexity of the dish.

Cultures: This type of fresh pasta, traditionally filled with potatoes, Sardinian pecorino cheese and mint, finds its ideal pairing in aromatic white wines, such as Vermentino di Gallura. With its vibrant acidity and citrus and floral notes, Vermentino balances the richness of the filling and highlights the freshness of the mint, creating an elegant and tasty pairing. Other interesting options include Nuragus di Cagliari, with its minerality and notes of white fruits, and Torbato di Alghero, with its unctuousness and aromas of Mediterranean herbs.

Fregula with Seafood: Fregula, a toasted semolina dough typical of Sardinia, prepared with fresh seafood and a touch of saffron, pairs well with white wines with good acidity and minerality, such as Vermentino di Gallura and Vernaccia di Oristano. The acidity of the wine cleanses the palate and enhances the flavor of the seafood, while the minerality complements the unctuousness of the dish. For those who prefer red wines, Monica di Sardegna, with its soft tannins and notes of red fruits, is an excellent option.

Seadas: This irresistible dessert, made with thin fried dough stuffed with fresh pecorino cheese and drizzled with honey, pairs well with sweet wines such as Malvasia di Bosa and Moscato di Sardinia. The sweetness and acidity of the wine balance the flavor of the cheese and honey, creating a perfect combination to finish the meal in style. Other sweet wines that can accompany seadas include Nasco di Cagliari and Vernaccia di Oristano Liquoroso.

Other Harmonizations:

- **Pane Carasau with Raw Ham and Pecorino Cheese:** This classic appetizer calls for a light, fruity red wine, like Monica di Sardegna or Cagnulari.
- **Malloreddus alla Campidanese:** This pasta dish with sausage and saffron sauce pairs well with full-bodied red wines, such as Cannonau Riserva or Carignano del Sulcis Superiore.
- **Gallura soup:** This bread, cheese and meat broth soup calls for a full-bodied white wine, such as Vermentino di Gallura Superiore or Vernaccia di Oristano Riserva.

The pairing between Sardinian cuisine and wines is an experience that awakens the senses and reveals the soul of the island. By combining the authentic flavors of traditional dishes with the richness and diversity of local wines, you can appreciate the essence of Sardinian culture and create memories that will last forever.

Tips for Tasting and Appreciation: Enjoying Sardinian Wines

Temperature: Serve red wines at room temperature (16-18°C) and white wines chilled (8-10°C).

Glasses: Use glasses suitable for each type of wine, to better appreciate its aromas and flavors.

Sensory analysis: Observe the color, aromas and flavors of the wine, perceiving its nuances and complexity.

Pairing: Try wines with local cuisine, for a complete experience.

Important Labels and Producers: Reference in Quality

Sardinia is home to a number of wineries and producers that stand out for their dedication to quality and the unique expression of the island's terroir.

- **Santadi winery:** One of Sardinia's most renowned wineries, Cantina di Santadi is known for its high-quality wines, such as "Terre Brune", made from the Carignano del Sulcis grape, and "Rocca Rubia", made from the Cannonau grape. Its wines are praised for their complexity, elegance and aging capacity.
- **Argiolas:** Argiolas is an iconic winery that produces wines that capture the essence of Sardinia. Its most famous wine, "Turriga", is made with the Cannonau grape and is considered one of the best red wines in Italy. Argiolas also produces other notable wines such as "Costamolino" (Vermentino) and "Korem" (Carignano).
- **Capichera:** Capichera specializes in the production of Vermentino di Gallura, a fresh and aromatic white wine that is the maximum expression of the Vermentino grape in Sardinia. Its "Capichera" wine is considered one of the best Vermentinos in Italy and is recognized for its minerality, vibrant acidity and citrus and floral aromas.
- **Sella & Mosca:** With a long history dating back to 1899, Sella & Mosca is one of the largest wineries in Sardinia. They produce a wide range of wines, from the classic "Alghero" (Cabernet Sauvignon and Merlot) to the fresh and vibrant "Vermentino di Sardegna". Sella & Mosca is known for its consistency and quality in all of its wines.

Awards and Recognition: Consecration of Sarda Excellence

Sardinian wines have gained recognition and prestige around the world, accumulating numerous awards and praise from specialized critics. Wines such as "Turriga" from Argiolas, "Terre Brune" from Cantina di Santadi and "Capichera" from Capichera are just a few examples of Sardinian wines that have won medals and high scores in international competitions.

These awards and recognitions are a testament to Sardinian producers' dedication to quality and the pursuit of excellence. They also help cement Sardinia's reputation as a world-class wine region, capable of producing wines that can compete with the best in the world.

A Treasure of Italian Viticulture

Sardinian wines represent a true treasure of Italian viticulture. With its rich history, unique indigenous grapes, diverse terroir and passionate producers, the island offers a unique and memorable wine experience.

Whether you're a lover of full-bodied red wines, fresh, aromatic whites or delicate rosés, Sardinia has something to offer. When you taste a Sardinian wine, you will be experiencing a piece of history, culture and passion that is reflected in every drop of this Mediterranean nectar.

Wine tourism in Sardinia: An Immersion in the Flavors and Charms of the Italian Island

Sardinia, the second largest island in the Mediterranean, is a paradise for wine and nature lovers. With stunning landscapes, rich history and culture, and unique cuisine, the island offers a complete and unforgettable wine tourism experience. In this detailed guide, we will explore Sardinia's attractions, wine tourism itineraries and experiences, wine-related events and festivals, and the importance of wine tourism for the local economy.

Island Attractions: A Feast for the Senses

Sardinia is a destination that captivates visitors with the diversity of its landscapes, the richness of its culture and the authenticity of its cuisine.

Breathtaking landscapes: The island offers a visual spectacle with its white sand beaches and crystal clear waters, rugged mountains, mysterious caves, archaeological sites and charming villages. The vineyards, spread throughout the island, complement the natural beauty, creating a perfect setting for wine lovers.

Ancient culture: Sardinia has a rich history and culture, with influences from different peoples who left their marks on the island. Nuraghi, megalithic constructions dating back to the Bronze Age, are one of the symbols of Sardinia. Folk festivals, traditional music and local crafts complement the cultural experience.

Authentic gastronomy: Sardinian cuisine is an explosion of flavors, with dishes that combine fresh and local ingredients, such as seafood, meats, cheeses, pastas and sweets. "Porceddu" (roasted suckling pig), "pane carasau" (thin, crispy bread) and "culurgiones" (a type of ravioli) are some of the island's specialties.

Wine Tourist Itineraries and Experiences: Discovering the Wines of Sardinia

Sardinia offers a variety of itineraries and wine tourism experiences for all tastes, from tastings at family wineries to guided tours through wine regions.

Wine regions: Explore the different wine regions of Sardinia, each with its own characteristics and grape varieties. Alghero, on the northwest coast, is known for its Vermentino white wines. Gallura in the north produces full-bodied red wines from Cannonau. The Cagliari region in the south offers a variety of red, white and rosé wines.

Winery visits: Discover Sardinia's wineries, from small family farms to large producers. Take part in guided tastings, learn about the production process and discover the secrets of the island's wines. Many wineries offer vineyard tours, paired lunches and other immersive experiences.

Tastings: Sample Sardinian wines in tastings guided by sommeliers. Discover the characteristics of each grape variety, the different styles of wine and the pairings with local cuisine.

Courses and workshops: Improve your knowledge about wine by participating in courses and workshops. Learn about the history of winemaking in Sardinia, tasting techniques and pairing with local cuisine.

Adventure wine tourism: Combine your passion for wine with outdoor activities. Go cycling or walking through the vineyards, explore the island by boat and enjoy spectacular views while tasting local wines.

Events and Festivals: Celebrating Wine Culture

Sardinia celebrates wine culture with various events and festivals throughout the year.

Calici di Stelle: A national event that takes place in August, during the night of San Lorenzo. Wineries open their doors for tastings, live music and stargazing.

Autunno in Barbagia: A festival that takes place from September to December, celebrating the culture and traditions of the Barbagia region. During the festival, villages open their homes and offer tastings of wine, local products and crafts.

Festa delle Cantine Aperte: An event that takes place in spring, when wineries open their doors to the public, offering tastings, guided tours and activities for the whole family.

The Importance of Wine Tourism for the Local Economy

Wine tourism has become increasingly important for Sardinia's economy. The activity generates jobs, income and development for the island, in addition to promoting the preservation of natural and cultural heritage.

Job creation: Wine tourism creates job opportunities in various sectors, such as hotels, gastronomy, transport and tourist services.

Economic diversification: Wine tourism contributes to the diversification of the local economy, which was traditionally based on agriculture and beach tourism.

Valuing culture: Wine tourism promotes the appreciation of Sardinian culture and traditions, encouraging the preservation of historical and cultural heritage.

Sustainability: Wine tourism encourages sustainable practices in wine production and tourism, contributing to the preservation of the environment.

In short, Sardinia offers a complete and authentic wine tourism experience, combining the natural beauty of the island with the richness of its culture, the tradition of its wines and the hospitality of its people. When visiting Sardinia, you will discover a destination that captivates the senses and invites you to immerse yourself in the flavors and charms of Italy.

Challenges and Perspectives for Sardinian Winemaking: Tradition and Innovation in a Unique Territory

Sardinia, an Italian island of wild beauty and rich history, cultivates an ancient winemaking tradition that dates back to Phoenician times. With a unique terroir, marked by the influence of the Mediterranean Sea and indigenous grape varieties, the island produces wines with its own identity, which express the essence of its territory. However, viticulture in Sardinia faces challenges and opportunities that require adaptation, innovation and a careful look at the future. In this text, we will explore the challenges and perspectives of viticulture in Sardinia, analyzing its potential to consolidate itself as a region producing excellent wines, with a focus on sustainability, research and the preservation of its cultural richness.

Production Challenges: Adapting to a Constantly Changing Scenario

Viticulture in Sardinia faces complex challenges that require innovative strategies and solutions to ensure the sustainability and competitiveness of the sector.

Climate change: Climate change represents a growing threat to viticulture around the world, and Sardinia is no exception. Rising temperatures, water scarcity, extreme weather events and the proliferation of diseases and pests affect the development of vines and the quality of grapes. Adapting to this new scenario requires the adoption of sustainable agricultural practices, the use of more resistant grape varieties and the development of mitigation and adaptation strategies.

Competition: The global wine market is highly competitive, and Sardinia faces competition from other producing regions in Italy and around the world. Differentiation through quality, typicality and appreciation of terroir is essential to conquer and maintain markets. Promoting Sardinian wines at national and international events, investing in marketing and building a strong brand are fundamental strategies for success in the global market.

Market: Changes in consumption habits, the search for cost-effective wines and growing competition in the domestic and foreign markets require Sardinian producers to adapt to new demands. The diversification of production, the exploration of new market niches, such as organic and biodynamic wines, and the strengthening of wine tourism are strategies to face market challenges.

Sustainability and Environmental Preservation: A Commitment to the Future

Environmental sustainability is an imperative for viticulture in Sardinia. The preservation of biodiversity, the protection of natural resources and the reduction of the environmental impact of production are fundamental to ensuring the longevity of the activity and the quality of life on the island.

Soil management: The adoption of soil management practices that preserve soil fertility and biodiversity, such as vegetation cover, direct planting and crop rotation, contributes to the sustainability of viticulture.

Water management: Water is a precious resource in Sardinia, and its efficient management is essential. The implementation of efficient irrigation systems, the reuse of rainwater and monitoring consumption contribute to water sustainability.

Biodiversity: The preservation of biodiversity in vineyards is fundamental to the balance of the ecosystem. The maintenance of natural areas, biological pest control and the responsible use of phytosanitary products contribute to the health of the vines and the quality of the grapes.

Renewable energy: The use of renewable energy sources, such as solar and wind energy, reduces dependence on fossil fuels and contributes to the reduction of greenhouse gas emissions.

Research and Innovation: Enhancing Tradition

Research and innovation play a fundamental role in Sardinian viticulture. The search for solutions to production challenges, adaptation to climate change, improving the quality of wines and valuing indigenous varieties drive innovation in the region.

Indigenous varieties: Sardinia has a wealth of native grape varieties, such as Cannonau, Vermentino and Carignano, which give its wines a unique identity. Research and clonal selection of these varieties aim to preserve the island's genetic heritage and improve the quality and adaptation of the grapes to local conditions.

Cultivation techniques: Research into cultivation techniques, such as pruning, management and disease control, seeks to optimize production, grape quality and vineyard sustainability.

Technology in winemaking: The incorporation of technology in winemaking, such as temperature control, micro oxygenation and the use of selected yeasts, allows the production of wines with greater complexity, elegance and typicality.

The Future of Winemaking in Sardinia: Challenges and Opportunities

Sardinia, with its unique terroir, indigenous grape varieties and a rich ancient winemaking tradition, has a promising future in the production of high quality wines. However, this future also presents considerable challenges.

Challenges:

- **Climate Change:** Viticulture is highly sensitive to climate change. Rising temperatures, water scarcity and extreme weather events can negatively impact grape production and quality. Adapting to these changes, through sustainable agricultural practices, selection of resistant varieties and investment in technology, is crucial for the survival and prosperity of the sector.
- **Global Competitiveness:** The global wine market is highly competitive. Sardinia needs to stand out, producing high quality wines, with unique identity and characteristics, that attract consumers and differentiate themselves from the competition.
- **Environmental Preservation:** Sustainable production, with respect for the environment, is increasingly valued by consumers. The adoption of agricultural practices that preserve biodiversity, soil quality and water is essential for the sustainability of the sector and for attracting conscious

consumers.

Opportunities:

- **Sustainability:** Investing in sustainable practices, such as organic and biodynamic agriculture, efficient water management and the use of renewable energy, can be a competitive differentiator for Sardinia, attracting consumers who value responsible production and respect for the environment.
- **Innovation:** Modern viticulture requires constant innovation. Investment in research and development, the adoption of new technologies and the improvement of production processes can increase the efficiency, quality and sustainability of the sector.
- **Valuation of indigenous varieties:** Sardinia's indigenous grapes, such as Cannonau, Vermentino and Carignano, represent a unique genetic heritage and offer the opportunity to produce wines with unique identity and characteristics, which stand out on the global market.
- **Strengthening Regional Identity:** Sardinia has a rich wine culture and tradition. Valuing this identity, through wine tourism, the creation of wine routes and the promotion of local gastronomy, can attract visitors and add value to the region's products.

The future of viticulture in Sardinia depends on the sector's ability to adapt to climate change, innovate, value its native varieties and strengthen its regional identity. The focus on sustainability, quality and typicality of Sardinian wines can consolidate the island as a region producing excellent wines, recognized worldwide.

Made in United States
North Haven, CT
07 June 2025

69599455R00026